Coordinator's Manual
Catholic Connections

Coordinator's Manual
Catholic Connections

Maura Thompson Hagarty
Brian Singer-Towns

Saint Mary's Press®

The publishing team included Maura Thompson Hagarty and Brian Singer-Towns, development editors; Lorraine Kilmartin, reviewer; Mary Lee Becker, compiler of appendix B; prepress and manufacturing coordinated by the production departments of Saint Mary's Press.

Copyright © 2009 by Saint Mary's Press, Christian Brothers Publications, 702 Terrace Heights, Winona, MN 55987-1318, www.smp.org. All rights reserved. Permission is granted to reproduce only the materials intended for distribution to catechists and parents. No other part of this manual may be reproduced by any means without the written permission of the publisher.

Printed in the United States of America

2250

ISBN 978-0-88489-740-8

Contents

1. Program Overview 6
2. Getting Started 10
3. Program Scheduling 17

Appendix A: Course Overviews

God, Revelation, and Faith 24

Jesus the Christ 26

The Holy Spirit and the Church 28

Sacraments and Prayer 30

The Eucharist 32

Christian Morality and Justice 34

Appendix B: Tip Sheets

Catechist Tip Sheet 1: Developmental Characteristics
    of Young Adolescents 37

Catechist Tip Sheet 2: Active Learning and Faith Formation 39

Catechist Tip Sheet 3: Effective Storytelling 41

Catechist Tip Sheet 4: Effective Group Management 43

Catechist Tip Sheet 5: Helping Young Adolescents
    to Pay Attention 45

Catechist Tip Sheet 6: Using the Scriptures 47

Parent Tip Sheet 1: Developmental Characteristics
    of Young Adolescents 49

Parent Tip Sheet 2: Three Key Family Faith Activities 51

Acknowledgments 53

Program Overview

Welcome to Catholic Connections! This is a parish religious education program for sixth, seventh, and eighth graders. Catholic Connections will strengthen the participants' Catholic identity and inspire them to participate more fully in the Church's mission. The sessions in the six courses will help young adolescents to make connections between the Catholic faith and everyday life and to strengthen their connection to the faith community.

The Components of the Catholic Connections Program

The program includes six fully developed courses, each with its own catechist guide full of active, hands-on learning sessions:

- God, Revelation, and Faith
- Jesus the Christ
- The Holy Spirit and the Church
- Sacraments and Prayer
- The Eucharist
- Christian Morality and Justice

In each course, the participants use as their textbook *The Catholic Connections Handbook for Middle Schoolers* (Saint Mary's Press, 2009). The handbook is a visually appealing, youth-friendly presentation of the Catholic faith. The learning sessions in the catechist guides work together with the handbook to equip parishes with an excellent resource for fostering the faith of young adolescents. Because the handbook has been declared in conformity with the *Catechism of the Catholic Church*, you can trust that its presentation of the faith is complete and authentic.

Correlation with the *Catechism of the Catholic Church*

The Catholic Connections program offers a comprehensive overview of the Catholic faith that is correlated with the four parts, or pillars, of the *Catechism of the Catholic Church*.

Catholic Connections Courses

Catechism of the Catholic Church

The Profession of Faith

The Celebration of the Christian Mystery

Life in Christ

Christian Prayer

The three courses that correspond to the Catechism's first pillar—God, Revelation, and Faith; Jesus the Christ; and The Holy Spirit and the Church—follow the *Catechism* by using the framework of the Creed to explore the central beliefs of Catholics. The *Catechism's* second pillar corresponds with two courses: Sacraments and Prayer and The Eucharist. An entire course is dedicated to the Eucharist because of its centrality and importance for the Catholic Church. The third pillar of the *Catechism* corresponds with the course Christian Morality and Justice. Prayer, the focus of the *Catechism's* fourth pillar, is explored in several sessions in the course Sacraments and Prayer as well as being integrated throughout the entire program.

"The whole concern of doctrine and its teaching must be directed to the love that never ends."[1] —Catechism of the Catholic Church

Why Just One Book for the Program Participants?

The Catholic Connections program features a single book for the participants for a number of reasons:

1. Comprehensive Overview

The Catholic Connections Handbook for Middle Schoolers offers a comprehensive overview of the Catholic faith in one handy volume. Providing young people with a one-volume overview helps to demonstrate that the Catholic faith is a unified, organic whole.

2. Maximum Program Flexibility

The Catholic Connections program is designed to suit a variety of program schedules and formats. Because the whole program is connected to just one participant handbook, coordinators can custom-design courses using material from multiple catechist guides without having to buy multiple participant books. See chapter 3 for more about scheduling options.

3. Personal Keepsake

Though the handbook is written specifically for sixth, seventh, and eighth graders, it is ungraded, meaning that a young person can keep it year after year and use it as his or her own personal guide to the Catholic faith.

4. Resource for Catechists

Because the course content is drawn from *The Catholic Connections Handbook for Middle Schoolers,* the handbook serves as a handy resource for catechists to use as they prepare for their sessions. The sessions include talking points for the catechists, but if catechists are able to do some additional reading in the handbook, they will be well prepared to summarize the doctrinal points covered by the sessions.

5. Vehicle for Connecting with Parents

If the participants have their own copies of the handbook and can take them home between sessions, the book has the potential to function as a bridge between parish and home. When the book goes home, parents have an informal opportunity to read about the topics their children are learning about or other topics of interest.

6. Anchor for the Catechetical Dimension of Other Aspects of Youth Ministry

Because it is just one volume, the handbook is easy to use in conjunction with programs such as retreats or service work that take place outside of formal religious education programs.

"While the catechesis offered within the family is ordinarily informal, unstructured, and spontaneous, it is no less crucial for the development of the child's faith."
— **National Directory for Catechesis**

Why Six 10-Session Courses?

The Catholic Connections program offers six courses, providing parishes with a large degree of flexibility. Parishes that offer three-year programs (sixth through eighth grade) may want to offer two courses per year, while parishes that offer two-year programs (seventh and eighth grade) may opt for three courses per year. The length of each course is also flexible, enabling parishes a variety of options for implementing the program. Each course offers a total of ten sessions: seven core sessions, two life issue sessions, and one concluding session designed with the option of including parents.

What You Will Find in This Manual

In the next chapter, you will find detailed descriptions of the features of the six courses in the Catholic Connections program. You will also find a checklist designed to help you implement the program.

Chapter 3 will walk you through a variety of scheduling options and offer guidance about course sequence.

Finally, the two appendices will provide you with a convenient way to share information with others. Appendix A provides overviews of the six courses. Appendix B provides tip sheets for catechists and parents on various topics related to the faith formation of young adolescents. Each course overview and each tip sheet is designed as a stand-alone reproducible handout, making it easy for you to share the information.

2 Getting Started

This chapter will help you get started with Catholic Connections. First it describes details about the program and course features. Then it describes specific "getting started" tasks and provides a checklist for your planning.

Features of Catholic Connections

Course Design

Each of the six Catholic Connections courses offers the following:
- seven core sessions
- two life issue sessions
- a concluding session
- an optional course project

Core Sessions

Each of the seven core sessions uses a chapter topic from *The Catholic Connections Handbook for Middle Schoolers* as a starting point and incorporates active learning strategies to help the participants understand the topic and explore its significance for their lives. The program as a whole provides forty-two core sessions.

Life Issue Sessions

The two life issue sessions in each course focus on issues that relate to young people's lives and explore those issues in light of material introduced during the seven core sessions. Both the core sessions and the life issue sessions aim to help the participants make important connections between the Catholic faith and their lives. The two types of sessions differ only in their starting points. The program as a whole provides twelve life issue sessions.

Concluding Session

Each course concludes with a tenth session that brings the course to a close and offers catechists the option of including the participants' parents. These sessions are designed to work effectively with or without parents in attendance.

"Catechesis most effectively promotes the faith development of . . . adolescents when the curriculum is focused on important faith themes drawn from the teachings of the Church and on the developmental needs and life experiences of adolescents." —Renewing the Vision

Optional Course Project

Each catechist guide includes detailed information about an optional course project. The primary aim of the course project is to help the participants synthesize what they are learning in the course and make connections between course material and their own lives. A secondary aim is to provide you and the catechists with a concrete way to involve parents in the young people's faith formation. Though the projects can be accomplished without parents, they are designed to give you and the catechists the option of having the participants work on aspects of the project at home in ways that may help parents connect with what their children are doing and learning. The projects do not put parents in the role of teacher; rather, they informally invite parents to learn along with their children.

The course projects are presented with a variety of options for implementation. It is best if the catechists start their courses already knowing how they want to use the project (e.g., at home, during sessions, with parents, without parents, in small groups) and when they want to introduce it (e.g., early in the course or midway through). The course overviews found in appendix A of this manual include brief descriptions of the course projects. Detailed project instructions for each course are located in the appendices of the respective catechist guides. Familiarize yourself with the projects and consider ways you can support the catechists who opt to use the course projects.

Time Frame for Sessions

The sessions in the six catechist guides are designed to work in periods of 60 to 75 minutes and include additional ideas for catechists working with longer time frames. According to our research, the vast majority of parish faith formation programs for sixth, seventh, and eighth graders meet weekly, and the sessions last for 60, 75, or 90 minutes. We responded to this by creating a program flexible enough to work well in a variety of time frames.

The Catholic Connections courses include fully designed 60-minute main sessions and 15-minute session extensions. In addition, the sessions include the following "extras" for groups with time frames longer than 75 minutes:

- *Discussion starters.* This feature offers two or three questions the catechists can use to encourage discussion.
- *Media connections.* This feature suggests movie clips, songs, or other media that can be used to further explore a session topic.
- *Optional course project.* The catechists who choose to use the optional course project can plan to incorporate some project work into the sessions.

Additional resources for extending sessions beyond 60 or 75 minutes are easy to find in *The Catholic Connections Handbook for Middle Schoolers*. Here are several suggestions:

- *"Think About It!"* Each chapter in the handbook has a "Think About It!" sidebar. The catechists can use these as the basis for discussion and reflection during sessions.
- *Images.* The handbook contains many images with captions well suited to sparking individual reflection and group discussion.
- *"People of Faith."* Over half the chapters in the handbook include "People of Faith" profiles and illustrations that depict key elements of the lives of faithful people. The catechists and the participants may enjoy exploring these during sessions.

The Catholic Connections program also has an optional card game called *GAME ON! Games for Catholic Connections* (Saint Mary's Press 2009), which contains cards with questions that can be used to play several kinds of games. One question on each card is specifically connected to each of the six courses. The catechists can use the card game to introduce or review course material with some lively and fun competition.

What's in Each Session?

Each session starts with a brief quick-start activity, usually lasting 5 minutes. These activities are largely self-directed, so as soon as the participants arrive they can jump right in. The opening prayer follows, and then the main part of the session begins.

The main part of each session aims to capture the participants' attention, help them to understand an aspect of Catholic teaching, and guide them in applying the teaching to their lives. The detailed session steps help the catechists to achieve these goals through a wide variety of approaches meant to relate to the many ways young people learn. These approaches or strategies include games, drama, physical movement, puzzles, crafts, role-playing, ritual, cooperative projects, lighthearted competition, field trips to the worship space, and simulations.

Most sessions are based on one or more chapters of *The Catholic Connections Handbook for Middle Schoolers*. At times the catechists are directed to involve the participants in looking at an image or reading a short section from the handbook. The catechist guides include images of many of the handbook pages that are referenced, making it easy for the catechists to work with the handbook and their guide at the same time.

The sessions also have the catechists summarize Church teaching for the participants. The guides provide talking points. The catechists are encouraged to review related material in the handbook as part of their preparation.

Each session also provides a closing prayer that usually includes a prayer found in the handbook. This makes it convenient for the catechists to invite everyone to say the same prayer together.

As mentioned earlier, the sessions include instructions for 15-minute optional session extensions. These are accompanied by notes about where they best fit into the overall session plans. The session extensions are designed to help the participants put an aspect of their faith into action.

"Catechetical methodology must exhibit a twofold fidelity. On the one hand, it must be faithful to God and to his Revelation; on the other, it must respect the liberty and promote the active participation of those being catechized."
— **National Directory for Catechesis**

Strategies for Helping Young People to Pay Attention

The catechist guides for the six Catholic Connections courses include strategies for helping the participants to pay attention during sessions. Capturing and keeping the attention of young adolescents can be a challenge for the catechists whether or not their groups include participants with diagnosed attention problems. The catechist guides use the following methods to help the catechists:

- *Background information.* The introduction to each guide includes a section that discusses attention issues, offers numerous easy-to-implement strategies, and identifies techniques to avoid. In addition, this manual includes a reproducible catechist tip sheet that summarizes this information (see appendix B). Encourage the catechists to spend some time reading and discussing this information with you before their courses begin or at times when group management issues may arise during the course.

- *Embedded strategies.* A number of strategies are embedded in the sessions themselves. An expert in the area of enhancing the attention of young learners reviewed the sessions and, when necessary, suggested changes to session plans that would help the catechists capture and hold the attention of the participants.

Reach Out to Parents

Parents play a critical role in the faith formation of their children, even when the young people have reached the middle school grades. Though the majority of the course sessions are designed for catechists meeting with the participants on their own, we encourage you to keep parents informed and to involve them whenever feasible. The Catholic Connections program offers you and the catechists a few concrete ways to reach out to parents:

- Send *The Catholic Connections Handbook for Middle Schoolers* home with the participants. This will give parents an informal way to learn along with their children and, ideally, this will spark family faith conversations.

- *Take advantage of intergenerational sessions.* The tenth and final session in each course is designed to accommodate parents. The sessions offer easy, concrete ways to include parents in the faith formation of their children without setting the parents up as teachers or experts.

- *Encourage catechists to implement course projects.* When young people have project-related tasks to do at home, let the parents know and ask them to support their children's efforts. When the projects come to an end, include parents in a celebration of the participants' work.

- *Distribute tip sheets and course overviews.* Share course overviews with parents so they have an idea about what their children are doing at the sessions. This manual includes reproducible handouts to make this easy (see appendix A). This manual also includes two reproducible tip sheets for parents, one on the developmental characteristics of young adolescents and the other on three key family faith activities: conversation, ritual, and service (see appendix B).

Checklist for Getting Started

Coordinator's Checklist

Task	Who Should Be Involved?	Completion Date
1. Determine schedule.	_____	_____
2. Secure meeting spaces.	_____	_____
3. Plan for special events.	_____	_____
4. Prepare registration materials.	_____	_____
5. Recruit catechists.	_____	_____
6. Train catechists.	_____	_____
7. Gather supplies.	_____	_____
8. Plan for evaluation.	_____	_____

1. Determine Schedule

Review the six courses and the information about scheduling options and course sequence (see chapter 3) and determine the schedule for your group's program.

2. Secure Meeting Spaces

Consider the number of courses you will offer at a particular time and the approximate number of participants who will be attending, and reserve the needed meeting spaces. Some courses include field trips to the worship space, so it would be ideal if your program could be held at a time when the worship space was available.

"Christian parents must strive to follow and repeat, within the setting of family life, the more methodical teaching received elsewhere." —Pope John Paul II

3. Plan for Special Events

If you opt to include parents in some sessions, and if you want to include end-of-course meals or celebrations, plan these early so everyone gets the dates on their calendars. If your circumstances allow, you may want to combine groups and have the catechists work together on end-of-course programs. If you offer two or three courses per year, you have two or three great opportunities for intergenerational celebrations.

4. Prepare Registration Materials

Maybe the better to way to think of this task is to prepare "invitations." Of course, it is important to convey all the times, dates, and deadlines to parents. If you can, though, consider sending invitations directly to the young people you hope to reach through your program.

5. Recruit Catechists

This is fifth in the list here, but ideally this is an ongoing effort throughout the year. Be on the lookout for parishioners who have the gifts to work effectively as catechists for middle school–aged youth. Even if you already have all the catechists you need, you can invite new recruits to participate in training and to shadow more experienced catechists for a year.

6. Train Catechists

Be prepared to gather your catechists and review the features of the courses and the catechist guides. Plan training opportunities that match the needs and experience levels of your catechists. Encourage the catechists to take advantage of additional opportunities offered by regional and diocesan catechetical leaders.

You may also want to make use of the reproducible catechist tip sheets located in appendix B of this manual. Topics include adolescent development, active learning, effective storytelling, effective group management, enhancing participants' attention, and using the Scriptures in faith formation.

7. Gather Supplies

Each session includes a "Materials Needed" section. Review these and determine which materials you will provide. Will you supply everything needed, or will you supply the basics and ask the catechists to gather special items? The basics include the following:

- a Bible
- copies of *The Catholic Connections Handbook for Middle Schoolers,* one for each participant
- pens or pencils, one for each participant
- a large blackboard, chalk, and an eraser; or a large whiteboard and markers
- supplies for creating a prayer space, such as a prayer table, a table covering, a Bible and stand, a cross, a candle and matches (if permitted)

Specialty items are those things that are used just once or infrequently. This might depend on how a catechist chooses to implement a particular activity. Please note that the supplies needed for the session extensions are listed separately just before the instructions for the extensions. This is so you and the catechists can keep track of what is needed for the main 60-minute portion of the sessions when you are not opting to do the extensions.

Some sessions provide the catechists with optional activities that require electronic equipment such as CD players and DVD players. Let the catechists know what kind of equipment is available to them.

8. Plan for Evaluation

From the start of your program, make plans for evaluation. Plan to seek input from the participants, the parents, and the catechists. You will learn things that will be invaluable for your program in the future.

Program Scheduling

The six courses in the Catholic Connections program provide an easy path in creating a two- or three-year program with weekly sessions. However, for those parishes using alternative scheduling formats, the six courses can be used to create programs that meet biweekly or monthly, or for retreat-based or weeklong programs. The structure of the sessions in each course allows for great flexibility in your scheduling.

This chapter suggests some possible scheduling formats, starting with those that are the most straightforward. Scheduling for the Sacrament of Confirmation is also considered, but first the sequence of the courses themselves are briefly discussed.

Sequence of Courses

As was mentioned in the first chapter, the Catholic Connections program offers an age-appropriate, comprehensive overview of the Catholic faith that aligns with the four pillars of the *Catechism of the Catholic Church*. The *Catechism* follows a specific logical order. In the first pillar, we are introduced to our Trinitarian God and how God has revealed himself to us, ultimately through the life, death, and Resurrection of Jesus Christ. We are also introduced to the Church, the living Body of Christ. In the second pillar, we are introduced to the liturgical and sacramental life of the Church. God's salvation, introduced in the first pillar, is made present through the liturgy and the sacraments. In the third pillar, the moral life is introduced. This follows the first two pillars because our moral life reflects the law of love revealed by God and is empowered by the sacraments. The fourth pillar introduces the importance of prayer in the life of the believer. A personal and communal prayer life is the foundation for coming to know God (first pillar), for growing in communion with the Trinity (second pillar), and for asking for the grace to live God's will (third pillar).

Thus, it follows that the most logical sequence for offering the courses in the Catholic Connections program is that which follows the order of the pillars of the *Catechism*:

1. God, Revelation, and Faith
2. Jesus the Christ
3. The Holy Spirit and the Church
4. Sacraments and Prayer
5. The Eucharist
6. Christian Morality and Justice

You can immediately see that the sequence is slightly interrupted with the sacraments and prayer being combined into a single course. This was intentional. Prayer is integrated into all the courses rather than being introduced through a single course, yet there are some sessions that focus specifically on prayer. This leads to an important catechetical principle: the content of catechesis is organic; that is, as we better understand the individual doctrines and fundamental concepts of our faith, we develop a deeper and richer understanding of our entire faith. The order in which we teach these concepts is not as important as is introducing all the major doctrines that make up our faith; thus, your pastoral and catechetical realities may be served better by an order that is different from the pillars of the *Catechism.*

So you should feel free to offer the Catholic Connections courses in whatever sequence makes the most sense in your parish situation. For example, if your students cover Christian morality in the year preceding your junior high program, you might decide to drop the Christian Justice and Morality course entirely from your junior high program. Or perhaps your parish has an intergenerational program that is focusing on the Eucharist for a year. So you may want to use The Eucharist course with all your middle school students in that year.

For simplicity, the following scheduling scenarios sequence the courses in the order that most directly follows the *Catechism.* But feel free to adapt this sequence in a way that makes the most sense in your pastoral situation.

> "*The* Catechism of the Catholic Church *is the doctrinal point of reference for education in the basic tasks of catechesis. However, it does not impose a predetermined format for the presentation of doctrine.*" —National Directory for Catechesis

Scheduling for Two- or Three-Year Programs with Weekly Meetings

In our research we found that most parish catechetical programs for middle school or junior high met once a week, from September through May. These are mostly three-year programs for grades six, seven, and eight, or two-year programs for grades seven and eight. Catholic Connections works with either two- or three-year programs, although you may be able to cover just the core sessions in a two-year program.

Three-Year Weekly Program Without Confirmation

A three-year program offers the simplest and most straightforward implementation of the Catholic Connections program. If your program groups young people by grade, you would offer all six courses every year, two courses each year for each grade. Your program schedule would look something like this:

	September	October	November	December	January	February	March	April	May
6th Grade	God, Revelation, and Faith					Jesus the Christ			
7th Grade	The Holy Spirit and the Church					Sacraments and Prayer			
8th Grade	The Eucharist					Christian Morality and Justice			

If your program groups young people in all three grades together, you would follow the same sequence except that you would offer just two courses each year on a three-year rotation.

Our research shows that most parish catechetical programs have twenty to thirty weekly meetings a year. This would allow you to offer all ten sessions in the two course pairings and still have meetings available for special liturgies, service projects, seasonal celebrations, and other special events.

Three-Year Weekly Program with Confirmation

More than a third of dioceses in the United States celebrate the Sacrament of Confirmation with junior high youth. If you add the immediate preparation for Confirmation to the spring of the eighth-grade year, your program schedule would look something like this:

	September	October	November	December	January	February	March	April	May
6th Grade	God, Revelation, and Faith					Jesus the Christ			
7th Grade	The Holy Spirit and the Church					Christian Morality and Justice			
8th Grade	Sacraments and Prayer and The Eucharist					Immediate Confirmation Preparation			

In this approach we recommend combining sessions from the Sacraments and Prayer course with sessions from The Eucharist course to create an introductory course on the sacraments preceding the immediate preparation for Confirmation. Because many Confirmation preparation programs contain sessions covering the Sacraments of Baptism, the Eucharist, and Confirmation, you can eliminate similar sessions from the Catholic Connections courses.

Two-Year Weekly Program Without Confirmation

A two-year program would require a little more planning, only because of the number of sessions the Catholic Connections program provides. You would offer three courses for each grade level each year, for a total of thirty sessions a year if you offered all ten sessions of each course. If your program does not meet thirty times, or if you use some of your meetings for sacramental celebrations and seasonal activities, you would still be able to provide a comprehensive exploration of the faith using the Catholic Connections program. By using only the seven core sessions of each course, you would still cover the essential content of each topic in twenty-one sessions. A program schedule organized in this manner would look something like this:

	September	October	November	December	January	February	March	April	May
7th Grade	God, Revelation, and Faith				Jesus the Christ			The Holy Spirit and the Church	
8th Grade	Sacraments and Prayer				The Eucharist			Christian Morality and Justice	

If you offer only the core sessions in your weekly meetings, the life issue sessions and the concluding session of each course could still be used as part of a retreat or in some other activity offered during the year.

Two-Year Weekly Program with Confirmation

As in the three-year program, we would recommend combining sessions from the Sacraments and Prayer course with sessions from The Eucharist course to create an introductory course on the sacraments preceding the immediate preparation for Confirmation. If the immediate preparation for Confirmation is in the spring of eighth grade, your program schedule would look something like this:

	September	October	November	December	January	February	March	April	May
7th Grade	God, Revelation, and Faith				Jesus the Christ			The Holy Spirit and the Church	
8th Grade	Christian Morality and Justice				Sacraments and Prayer and The Eucharist			Immediate Confirmation Preparation	

Scheduling for Programs with Non-Weekly Formats

Though weekly meetings are most common for middle school religious education programs, many parishes have found success with other scheduling approaches. Because Catholic Connections uses a single handbook and flexible sessions in its courses, it can be adapted to work with almost any schedule and setting. This section describes three alternatives to spark your own creative thinking.

Biweekly, Monthly, and Quarterly Models

Some parishes have found that meeting less frequently for longer periods of time is an effective response to the challenge of the busy lives of young people, their families, and catechists. This may mean meeting once or twice a month on a Saturday morning or Sunday afternoon, or offering a quarterly weekend catechetical retreat. Parishes have found that an added benefit to this model is the deeper sense of community the participants experience.

Should your program meet every other week or twice a month for two or more hours, you could complete a course in ten weeks by combining two course sessions each time you meet. Your schedule would look very much like the schedules for weekly meetings, shown earlier.

In implementing a model of daylong or weekend meetings, you would focus on a particular catechetical topic during these longer experiences. You would use the Catholic Connections course sessions on that topic as your core experiences in building the schedule for the day or weekend. As part of the day or weekend, you would also plan additional community-building activities, prayer opportunities, meals, and even sacramental celebrations to create a more retreat-like atmosphere.

Summer Program Model

The summer months offer a unique opportunity to provide catechetical programming for middle schoolers. Vacation Bible programs for elementary-age children are already popular. Providing a similar weeklong experience for middle schoolers takes advantage of their availability during the weekdays. It also provides a safe and positive experience for young people while their parents are at work. And you have opportunities to take the young people on daylong field trips to nearby places for fun and service.

In creating such a summer program, you would focus on one or possibly two courses. The week will provide opportunities to cover most if not all the sessions in a course. Throughout the week you would also build in time for prayer, games, service projects, and a fun day. A schedule for a summer middle school week might look something like this:

	Monday	Tuesday	Wednesday	Thursday	Friday
AM	Welcome Community-building games Session 1	Morning prayer Session 4 Snacks Session 5	Morning prayer Session 6 Snacks Session 7	Morning prayer All day fun activity • theme park • water park • science center	Morning prayer Morality service project
PM	Lunch Gym or outdoor activities Session 2 Snacks Session 3	Lunch Afternoon service project	Lunch Movie Session 8		Lunch Session 9 Session 10 Review games Closing prayer and celebration

Intergenerational Model

Many parishes in the United States are looking at, or have already implemented, intergenerational models for faith formation. Typically, intergenerational programs gather parishioners of all ages at the same session; often these are monthly gatherings. The sessions focus on particular aspects of Catholic teaching, and everyone participates in common prayer time and activities, but usually there is also breakout time for age-specific catechesis on the topic. In addition to these intergenerational sessions, parishes supply take-home materials for families, and some also offer additional grade-specific catechetical programming on the topic.

Catholic Connections is a useful resource for the age-specific component of intergenerational programs because of the single, ungraded handbook and the overview of the faith in the six courses. With the comprehensive content in *The Catholic Connections Handbook for Middle Schoolers,* the participants and their families can follow whatever topic is selected for the intergenerational program. And the sessions in the six courses are excellent resources for those leading the catechesis for young people in the age-level breakouts and additional meetings.

Appendix A
Course Overviews

God, Revelation, and Faith	24
Jesus the Christ	26
The Holy Spirit and the Church	28
Sacraments and Prayer	30
The Eucharist	32
Christian Morality and Justice	34

Overview of God, Revelation, and Faith Course

Throughout these sessions the young people will address the basic questions of who God is and how we come to know God. They will be presented with the understanding of God as Father, Son, and Holy Spirit, who is revealed through Sacred Tradition and the Sacred Scriptures. The participants will also explore the meaning of our human existence and how God is actively involved in the work of our salvation. Though it is God who saves us, the young people will be challenged to do their part: respond to God with faith.

Course Themes

Core Session: 1. Revelation, the Scriptures, and Tradition

This session explores how God reveals himself to us, focusing on the two main modes of God's Revelation: the Scriptures and Tradition.

Core Session: 2. God the Father

This session examines God the Father and how he has revealed himself to us.

Core Session: 3. The Holy Trinity

This session delves into the mystery of the Holy Trinity and how our one God is the union of three unique Persons.

Core Session: 4. Creation

This session looks at God's creativity at work in our world, explores the biblical story of the fall of humanity, and considers how we all must make choices between good and evil.

God, Revelation, and Faith Overview: Permission to reproduce is granted. © 2009 by Saint Mary's Press.

Core Session: 5. The Human Person

This session investigates what it means to be made in the image of God and examines how Original Sin has affected humanity.

Core Session: 6. God's Plan for Salvation

This session examines the ways God has guided humanity throughout salvation history, recognizing how God continues to lead his people back to be with him, their ultimate home.

Core Session: 7. Faith: Responding to God

This session examines the three elements of faith that are being taught and explores the faith of some of the greatest figures in the Bible.

Life Issue Session: 8. Who Am I?

This session helps to identify the commonalities and differences among young people and also provides the groundwork to get past the superficial ways young people identify themselves. It also explores a number of Scripture passages to help us discover who we are according to God.

Life Issue Session: 9. Winning and Losing

This session offers a different perspective on winning and losing. It examines the Beatitudes and other biblical passages to see how people embody God's Word in their own lives and then challenges the participants to come up with ways they can live out these Gospel values.

Concluding Session: 10. Salvation History

This concluding session focuses on how God has interacted with humanity throughout history, offering the participants an opportunity to reflect on how God continues to interact with them in their own lives through the events and people of their lives.

Optional Course Project: My Salvation History

This project is designed to enable the participants to see how God acts through the events they experience and through the people they have relationships with.

Overview of Jesus the Christ Course

Christ stands at the center of salvation history, at the center of our parishes, and in the hearts of all believers. Throughout these sessions the participants will come to know the many faces of Jesus. They will meet the Jesus of the Gospels, finding the relationship between his story and their own. They will explore the other sources that connect us to Christ, including the Church, their parents, and their peers. Care will be taken to be sure they understand important Christological concepts such as Jesus' Incarnation, the Trinity, Jesus' miracles, and salvation.

Throughout these sessions the young people will be challenged to rely on Jesus as our Savior, a role model, a teacher, a caregiver, and a guide. The participants will have the opportunity to enter into a deeper understanding and relationship with our Lord, from Jesus' humble earthly beginnings to his glorious Resurrection, recognizing that their lives are centered in God.

Course Themes

Core Session: 1. The Gospels

This session looks at Jesus as he is presented in the Gospels. The session recognizes the diversity in the Gospel stories and underscores the saving truth of the Scriptures through the inspiration of the Holy Spirit.

Core Session: 2. Jesus Christ, True God and True Man

This session explores who Jesus is, how we find out more about him, and who we are in relationship to him.

Core Session: 3. The Birth of Jesus

This session explores Jesus' birth, especially the mystery of the Incarnation, in which the Son of God became flesh and dwelt among us.

Jesus the Christ Overview: Permission to reproduce is granted. © 2009 by Saint Mary's Press.

Core Session: 4. Jesus Teaches

This session looks at Jesus' role as teacher and guide. Some of Jesus' parables are studied to see what they teach us today.

Core Session: 5. Jesus Heals

This session presents Jesus as a true superhero who could truly work miracles and change the world. The participants are challenged to see where Christ's healing still is needed today.

Core Session: 6. The Death of Jesus

This session looks at Jesus' death by praying the stations of the cross. The saving nature of Jesus' death is presented.

Core Session: 7. The Resurrection of Jesus

By role-playing a talk show, the participants look at the impact Jesus' Resurrection had on his followers. Christ's Resurrection is presented as the basis for our hope of salvation and eternal life.

Life Issue Session: 8. Friends in Jesus

This session looks at what we can learn from Jesus about being a good friend. The participants will practice bringing Jesus' values into their friendships.

Life Issue Session: 9. Times of Trouble

The participants will consider the help Jesus brings us during times of trouble. They will be encouraged to rely on prayer, parents, and peers; these are some ways we experience Christ's love and support during difficult times.

Concluding Session: 10. One Body, Many Parts

This session focuses on having gratitude for the gifts God has given us and on the responsibility to follow Jesus' example in using those gifts in the service of others.

Optional Course Project: The Many Faces of Jesus

The participants will gather images of Jesus and choose an artistic way to present them to the rest of the community.

Overview of
The Holy Spirit and the Church Course

The Holy Spirit energizes and brings life to the Church and to all baptized believers. Throughout these sessions the participants will explore how the Holy Spirit moves in God's people and will discover concrete ways that the Holy Spirit is present in the world today. They will examine how the gift of God's grace is made possible by the Spirit and what it means to be invited to participate in God's life. The participants will reflect on the Gifts of the Holy Spirit and how these gifts help them to respond to God's love. In exploring the Holy Spirit's activity in the Church, the young people will look at how God's Spirit was present in the lives of the Apostles, examine various models that help us to understand the meaning of Church, and look at how all the baptized participate in the mission of Christ to make disciples of all nations. The remaining sessions focus on what is needed to enter God's Kingdom and how Mary, the saints, and those whose lives reflect the qualities, values, and beliefs that characterize Jesus' followers can serve as models of faithful discipleship.

Course Themes

Core Session: 1. The Holy Spirit

This session explores how the Holy Spirit is present in the world today and gives life to the mission of Jesus Christ.

Core Session: 2. Grace and the Gifts of the Holy Spirit

This session examines the gift of God's grace and how it allows us to participate in the life of God and enables us to bring God's love to others.

Core Session: 3. Pentecost and the Early Church

This session looks at the Holy Spirit's activity in the early Church. The session recognizes that the coming of the Holy Spirit on the Apostles at Pentecost marked the beginning of the Church and empowered Jesus' disciples to spread the Good News to the ends of the earth.

The Holy Spirit and the Church Overview: Permission to reproduce is granted. © 2009 by Saint Mary's Press.

Core Session: 4. The Mission of the Church

This session examines how images of the Church, specifically the People of God, the Body of Christ, and the Temple of the Holy Spirit, help us to understand the nature of the Church community.

Core Session: 5. The Structure of the Church

This session explores how all baptized Catholics are called to participate in the mission of Christ to make disciples of all nations by participating in the priestly, prophetic, and kingly mission of Christ.

Core Session: 6. End Things: Heaven and Hell

This session reflects on God's desire for us to be with him and how choosing to follow Jesus' command to love others can lead to perfect union and happiness with God forever.

Core Session: 7. Saints and Mary

This session explores the special connection that we have with Mary and the saints and how they are examples for us of what it means to be disciples of Jesus.

Life Issue Session: 8. Dealing with Peer Pressure

This session examines how peer pressure can be either positive or negative. The session emphasizes the role of the Holy Spirit in helping young people deal with peer pressure and helps them develop the skills and tools needed to resist negative peer pressure.

Life Issue Session: 9. Role Models: Whom Should I Look Up To?

This session explores how role models help us become the people we want to be and how to identify the qualities and values characteristic of Christian role models.

Concluding Session: 10. The Holy Spirit and the Church Celebration

This session revisits some of the main themes of the previous sessions and allows the young people (and, optionally, their parents) to celebrate what they have learned and the time they have spent together.

Optional Course Project: The Spirit Is Moving All Around Us!

The participants will look for signs of the Holy Spirit at work in the world around them: in their families, parish, and community.

Overview of Sacraments and Prayer Course

This course is designed to help young people better understand and more fully participate in the Church's sacraments and prayer life. The sessions connect directly to *The Catholic Connections Handbook for Middle Schoolers* and cover basic teachings about the sacraments and prayer. The participants will begin with an overview of the Church's Seven Sacraments and then explore the sacraments in more detail. They will also explore the topic of prayer and address two life issues relevant to young people in light of course material. The importance of the central place of the Eucharist in Catholic life will also be emphasized.

Course Themes

Core Session: 1. Sacraments: Celebrating Christ's Presence

This session introduces the participants to the Seven Sacraments and how they help us to recognize the invisible reality of Christ's presence.

Core Session: 2. The Eucharist

This session looks at the Church's central sacrament, the Eucharist, and provides the participants with an overview.

Core Session: 3. Baptism and Confirmation

This session uses a sports metaphor to explore Baptism and Confirmation and how the Church initiates new members.

Core Session: 4. The Sacraments of Healing

This session helps to increase the participants' familiarity with the Sacraments of Penance and Reconciliation and Anointing of the Sick so that they will be comfortable asking for them when they, a friend, or a family member would benefit from them.

Sacraments and Prayer Overview: Permission to reproduce is granted. © 2009 by Saint Mary's Press.

Core Session: 5. Matrimony and Holy Orders

This session provides an overview of the Church's two Sacraments of Service and encourages the participants to consider how they can use their gifts to serve others.

Core Session: 6. Prayer: Tuning In to God

This session focuses on God's constant presence and desire for relationship with us. It encourages the participants to consider ways they can tune in to God's presence.

Core Session: 7. The Lord's Prayer

This session looks at the meaning of the Lord's Prayer and involves the participants in exploring the prayer's seven petitions.

Life Issue Session: 8. The Ultimate Question: Why Am I Here?

This session draws on course material to help the participants explore one of life's big questions and encourages the participants to recognize that they were created with a God-given purpose.

Life Issue Session: 9. God, Where Are You?

This session focuses on finding God when God seems far away and considers how helpful the Church's sacraments and prayer can be.

Concluding Session: 10. The Eucharist in Catholic Life

The final session returns to the topic of the Eucharist and emphasizes its central place in the life of the Church.

Optional Course Project: Project Global Connect

By collecting and reviewing parish bulletins from around the nation and world, the participants will learn how their home parish's sacrament and prayer practices are linked to the global Catholic Church family.

Overview of The Eucharist Course

Each session of this course examines a part or aspect of the Eucharist. The sessions help the participants uncover the deeper, hidden meanings that can be found in the concrete, tangible symbols of the Mass.

The opening session teaches the participants how to read liturgical symbols with the eyes of faith so they can peel away each layer to discover the mystery of Christ within. Then the following sessions examine the primary symbols and actions of the Eucharist to show how our praying together in memory of Jesus teaches us about our faith and how to live it in the world. Through these sessions and the participants' own experience of the Eucharist, you will be able to catechize about the meaning of thanksgiving, proclamation, intercession, imagination, procession, sacrifice, prayer and blessing, time and movement, breaking and sharing, mission, commitment, and service.

The Eucharist catechizes us. In turn when you begin to catechize through the experience of the Eucharist, you will help the young people discover the wonder and awe of this prayer of the Church and its meaning for their lives.

Course Themes

Core Session: 1. Introduction to Liturgy

This session introduces the participants to the nature of liturgy and underscores how we see God through the symbols and actions of the liturgy.

Core Session: 2. The Eucharist: The Heart of All Liturgy

This session introduces the participants to the Eucharist and helps them understand that celebrating the Eucharist is a way we express our thanks to God.

Core Session: 3. The Liturgy of the Word

This session explores the Liturgy of the Word and presents the Scriptures proclaimed at Mass as a living Word.

The Eucharist Overview: Permission to reproduce is granted. © 2009 by Saint Mary's Press.

Core Session: 4. The Liturgy of the Eucharist: Using Our Gifts

This session, the first of two on the Liturgy of the Eucharist, focuses on the Preparation of the Gifts and explores the meaning of offering, gift, and sacrifice.

Core Session: 5. The Liturgy of the Eucharist: The Power of Prayer

This session, the second of two on the Liturgy of the Eucharist, focuses on the Eucharistic Prayer, the Church's principal prayer of thanksgiving to God. The session draws the participants' attention to their roles in the prayer.

Core Session: 6. Communion

This session explores Communion and how it leads us to mission.

Core Session: 7. Sending Forth

This session presents the dismissal as a commissioning and explores how the Eucharist sends us out to serve others.

Life Issue Session: 8. Family

This session helps the participants understand the nature of family relationships and guides them in visualizing the Church as a family gathered around the Eucharistic table.

Life Issue Session: 9. Time

The participants consider how they use their time and relate it to the concepts of *chronos* and *kairos*. The session highlights that time spent celebrating sacraments is special because of God's unique presence. It also points out that we can recognize the special quality of all our time if we keep our eyes open to God's constant presence and love.

Concluding Session: 10. Take, Bless, Break, Share

In the final session, the participants work together to create a ritual prayer by preparing four different prayer elements: word, music, environment, and movement.

Optional Course Project: Preparing a Mealtime Prayer

The participants will prepare a mealtime prayer that can be used at an additional gathering in place of session 10, or in their family homes.

Overview of Christian Morality and Justice Course

Christian morality is built on God's steadfast call to live in right relationship with God and with others. God has given us the Ten Commandments as a guide for living in right relationship. This course will help the participants to learn about the moral principles embodied in the Ten Commandments. In each core session, the young people will explore one or more of the Ten Commandments. The participants will have opportunities to apply these Christian moral principles to various real-life situations and will be encouraged to use those principles in their own daily lives. They will examine their own experiences and consider many of the moral dilemmas young people often face. In particular, the two life issue sessions apply the Ten Commandments to the important issues of how we use our money and how we use technology.

Course Themes

Core Session: 1. Moral Decision Making

This session helps the participants to consider their own decision-making processes and to learn to use the Cardinal Virtues as tools for making good decisions.

Core Session: 2. Honoring God

This session explores God's power and role as Creator. The participants will learn that the First Commandment calls us to honor God for all God's great deeds.

Core Session: 3. Honoring Family

This session explores the role parents play in young people's lives and the Fourth Commandment's call to honor our parents.

Christian Morality and Justice Overview: Permission to reproduce is granted. © 2009 by Saint Mary's Press.

Core Session: 4. Respecting Life

This session explores the presence of God's image in all of us and the Fifth Commandment's call to respect all life.

Core Session: 5. Respecting Truth and Property

This session explores the effects that lying and stealing have on relationships. The participants will learn that the Seventh and Eighth Commandments help us to develop trusting relationships.

Core Session: 6. Respecting Sexuality

This session explores the messages from our culture about sexuality and sex. The participants will learn that the Sixth Commandment protects God's true purposes for sex.

Core Session: 7. Working for Justice

This session explores the young people's desire for fairness and how that desire can lead them to answer God's call to do acts of charity and works of justice.

Life Issue Session: 8. Using Money

This session explores the differences between wants and needs. The participants will learn that God calls us to set priorities and use our money wisely, keeping those differences in mind.

Life Issue Session: 9. Using Technology

This session explores how using technology involves making moral choices. The participants will learn that God calls us to use technology in ways that develop good relationships with God and others.

Concluding Session: 10. Reaching God's Goal for Our Lives

This session explores how attaining goals involves choices. The participants will understand that we are to make God's goal—of living in right relationship with God and others—our own personal goal as well.

Optional Course Project: Morality and the Movies

The participants will watch a movie and analyze it based on the general moral principles they have learned during the course.

Appendix B
Tip Sheets

*Catechist Tip Sheet 1: Developmental Characteristics
  of Young Adolescents* 37

Catechist Tip Sheet 2: Active Learning and Faith Formation 39

Catechist Tip Sheet 3: Effective Storytelling 41

Catechist Tip Sheet 4: Effective Group Management 43

*Catechist Tip Sheet 5: Helping Young Adolescents
  to Pay Attention* 45

Catechist Tip Sheet 6: Using the Scriptures 47

*Parent Tip Sheet 1: Developmental Characteristics
  of Young Adolescents* 49

Parent Tip Sheet 2: Three Key Family Faith Activities 51

CATECHIST
Tip Sheet 1

Developmental Characteristics of Young Adolescents

Adolescence is a critical time of identity formation. With the onset of puberty comes an explosion of growth of many kinds: physical, intellectual, emotional, social, moral, and spiritual. Understanding the nature and scope of adolescent development and responding appropriately requires patience, empathy, and a sense of humor. Young people "progress" through adolescence, no two following the same pathway. Most sixth graders show signs of emerging traits, while many eighth graders exhibit more pronounced characteristics. The characteristics listed on this tip sheet are descriptors, not predictors.

Physical

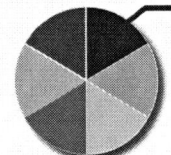

- experience onset of puberty, develop secondary sex characteristics
- grow rapidly, are often clumsy and uncoordinated
- become highly self-conscious, body image can affect self-image
- fluctuate between hyperactivity and lethargy
- need physical activity

Cognitive-Intellectual

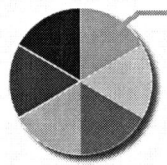

- develop ability to think abstractly, but many still think in literal terms
- develop critical thinking skills and become more self-aware, self-critical
- exhibit increased communication skills
- become argumentative and demonstrate an intense need to be "right"
- develop decision-making skills and want a voice in their choices
- show intense focus on a new interest but lack discipline to sustain it

Emotional

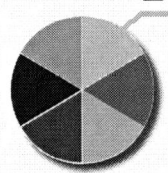

- are unpredictable emotionally, are sensitive and prone to outbursts
- are vulnerable to emotional pleas and can be easily manipulated
- exhibit an increasing capacity for empathy
- experience increasing sexual feelings, may engage in sexual behavior without realizing consequences

Catechist Tip Sheet 1: Permission to reproduce is granted. © 2009 by Saint Mary's Press.

Catechist Tip Sheet 1 • Page 2

Social-Interpersonal

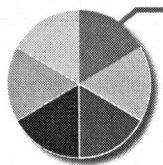

- display a more developed social consciousness
- are more aware of relationships and have a strong need to belong
- exhibit desire for independence and autonomy
- experience a shift in dependence on family to dependence on peers
- able to critically compare parents with others
- seek deeper friendships based on shared interests, loyalty
- experience increased interest in opposite sex, though may often feel uncomfortable and awkward with the other sex

Moral

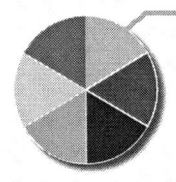

- tend to be legalistic, focusing on "rules" and "fairness"
- retain moral beliefs of parents but begin to test rules of childhood
- are influenced by the values of peers
- form a more personal conscience, seek moral criteria that make sense to them
- exhibit a stronger sense of responsibility toward larger society

Spiritual

- exhibit "affiliative faith" (faith identity shaped by family and community)
- are open to service opportunities primarily to connect with peers, test skills
- can be open to new prayer experiences
- seek adult role models who live their faith authentically
- desire a deeper relationship with God
- begin moving away from religious imagery, beliefs, and practices of childhood; may begin to explore new images of God

Being a Catechist and Mentor

- Consider the young people in your group and the six areas of growth. In which areas are they strong? struggling? How can you support their growth?

- Recall what it was like to be their age. What is it like for them today? How can you relate? What is different?

- Years from now, when they reflect on these times with you, how will the young people remember you? How will their time with you help to shape their identity and beliefs?

Catechist Tip Sheet 2

Active Learning and Faith Formation

Experience is the best teacher. Once you learn to ride a bike, you never forget—not because you read about it, but because you did it. It is difficult to forget something learned through experience.

People tend to learn least through "passive" methods like reading textbooks or listening to lectures. Active methods, involving direct, meaningful, and personal experiences, are most effective.

This chart compares the characteristics of active learning with those of traditional passive learning. The distinctions have been somewhat exaggerated for clarity.

Passive Learning Characteristics	Active Learning Characteristics
Learners start by receiving the content of what is to be learned.	Students start by sharing an experience.
Teachers and catechists are the givers of information; students are receptacles for information.	Students are actively involved in discovering what is to be learned from the experience; teachers are guides and resources, facilitating the process.
The learning process is deductive. It starts with general principles and moves to particular application.	The learning process is inductive. It starts with a particular experience and moves to a general principle.
The learning environment is orderly, quiet, controlled. Adolescent energy is resisted and restricted.	The learning environment is occasionally noisy and chaotic but still controlled. Adolescent energy is channeled and engaged in discovery.
Students infrequently move or interact.	Students frequently move and interact.
Discussion is used to ensure that the students have memorized the content.	Discussion is used to explore the meaning of a particular experience and to apply new knowledge to life situations.

Catechist Tip Sheet 2: Permission to reproduce is granted. © 2009 by Saint Mary's Press.

Active learning captures the attention and involves the learner. Through games, role-plays, simulations, hands-on activities, and inductive discovery, the learner is engaged not just on a cognitive level but on a number of levels. Active methods are well suited to faith formation sessions with young adolescents. Here are some strategies for effective facilitation:
- Study the characteristics of active learning.
- Practice leading active faith formation activities.
- Allow adequate time, as active methods can require extra preparation steps.
- Avoid the temptation to skip activities that may appear superfluous at first.

Through active learning, "religion" moves beyond mere memorization. Teachers become facilitators of learning, students become explorers of meaning, and faith is brought to life!

An Example of Active Learning
Being Part of the Body of Christ

1. Divide the large group into small groups of six, and give each young person two or three playing cards.

2. Instruct the small groups to build a two-story card house, each group member adding one card at a time. If a group's house collapses, the group members take their cards back and the group starts over.

3. Ask the participants to identify connections they see between building the house and living as the Body of Christ. Incorporate the following ideas if the participants do not identify them:
- Each person has different cards, but all are equally important to the common goal.
- The choices individuals make have an impact on the whole group.
- When things go wrong, it helps to work together and try again.
- Different talents are needed at different stages—creativity, patience, encouragement, and so on.

4. Read aloud 1 Corinthians 12:12–13.

5. Offer concluding comments that build on the participants' experience and ideas and that recap the main idea of the passage that the Body of Christ is made up of many members who are united by the Spirit.

CATECHIST Tip Sheet 3

Effective Storytelling

Stories are often the best way to capture and convey the power of deep truths and significant relationships. Consider how people are enamored when someone tells the story of meeting and falling in love with his or her spouse or recalls the birth of his or her first child.

As Catholics we are storytellers at heart. We retell the stories of faith passed from one generation to the next through the Scriptures and personal life experiences. Our stories of faith express the deep love relationship we have with God.

Jesus himself is the Story of God, the Word of God proclaimed most fully. We believers have our own stories of faith to tell as well; we too are words of God. When we share our faith with young people, we hope they will also become truly fascinated with Jesus.

If we want our sessions to come alive with genuine passion and enthusiasm, we must tell stories—stories of our own faith encounters with God, stories of how we have learned what it means to be a follower of Jesus, stories of our experiences with other people of faith. We will tell stories that are funny, sad, poignant, even occasionally embarrassing. And when we tell these stories with honesty and enthusiasm, the spiritual imagination is ignited!

In hearing stories, young people will discover that they too have wonderful stories to share. And each time a story of faith is told, the Good News is proclaimed once again.

Young people enjoy a wide variety of stories—folktales, fairy tales, myths, parables, contemporary tales—but the most powerful stories are often personal ones that recount significant experiences.

> Young people enjoy a wide variety of stories—folktales, fairy tales, myths, parables, contemporary tales—but the most powerful stories are often personal ones that recount significant experiences.

Catechist Tip Sheet 3: Permission to reproduce is granted. © 2009 by Saint Mary's Press.

Hints for Sharing Your Stories

The following suggestions are intended to help you tell stories about your experiences during faith formation sessions:

- Make sure your story has a clear lesson and purpose. When selecting a life story, ask yourself what you have personally experienced that relates to the point you wish to convey.

- Make sure your story fits in with the rest of the session plan. If it is presented out of context, it will lose its effect.

- Give your story time to develop. Details are vital and can bring the story to life! Include descriptions of the atmosphere, location, and people involved. But do not drag the story out too much; this may cause it to lose its effectiveness.

- Let the tone of your story fit the purpose of the session. Tell it in a way that creates an atmosphere that enhances the learning. For example, avoid telling a humorous story right before prayer.

- Always make explicit the feeling level of your story. Good stories touch the heart, not just the head. But remember that young adolescents are emotionally vulnerable; take care not to manipulate their feelings.

- Be authentic. Young people will detect and reject phoniness immediately.

- Practice your story! Usually if a good story does not go over well, it simply needs better telling. Try different approaches, expressions, or punch lines. A good story deserves to be told well.

- At the conclusion of the story, clearly state the lesson to be learned. Do not presume the participants will get the point without explanation.

- Stories should be personal, but this does not mean you should pour out your deepest secrets to the young people. To assure appropriate boundaries of self-disclosure, first tell your story to a friend and ask for feedback.

CATECHIST Tip Sheet 4

Effective Group Management

Effective group management is grounded in positive relationships of mutual respect between catechists and participants and among group members. Viewing young adolescents in a positive light requires dispelling stereotypes that portray them as uncontrollable, disrespectful, and rude. When programs for young people are well conceived, age appropriate, and directed by capable and caring adults, behavior problems are minimized.

Initially you may find that the young people are being forced to attend the program, which can contribute to negative attitudes and behaviors. However, as relationships develop and the participants experience positive program activities, their enthusiasm will grow, as will their cooperation.

As with any group, two dynamics are at play, and sometimes are in tension: the *task* to accomplish (the lesson) and the *relationships* among the members (how youth interact with one another). You will need to tend to both of these functions in order to manage the group. Two basic principles should guide you:

Principle 1
Be well prepared to facilitate each session. If you are confident and comfortable with the lesson plan, you will be relaxed and more able to focus on the young people.

Principle 2
Whenever encountering the participants, focus on building positive relationships. Get to know the young people, take an interest in their lives, be affirming, and let them know you care.

- Be well prepared to facilitate each session. If you are confident and comfortable with the lesson plan, you will be relaxed and more able to focus on the young people.

- Whenever encountering the participants, focus on building positive relationships. Get to know the young people, take an interest in their lives, be affirming, and let them know you care.

Catechist Tip Sheet 4: Permission to reproduce is granted. © 2009 by Saint Mary's Press.

Techniques for Preventing Disruptive Behavior

The following techniques will help you not only to resolve but to avoid altogether the vast majority of discipline issues:

- Maintain appropriate expectations. Young people will live up—or down—to the expectations you set. Base expectations on the developmental characteristics of this age-group. In other words, expect them to be precisely who they are—adolescents—and be ready to love and enjoy them as they are.

- Establish clear boundaries. Make them simple, reasonable, and to the point. Young people need to know the limits. Explain exactly what the guidelines are and what they mean—describe what *respect* means, don't presume the young people know! Basic guidelines could include the following:
  - ▶ Respect people and property.
  - ▶ Be positive and participate fully.
  - ▶ Only one person speaks at a time.
  - ▶ No put-downs.
  - ▶ Behave properly, particularly during prayer times.

- Explain clearly the consequences of broken rules. Impose them quickly and uniformly. If the young people learn that established guidelines for behavior can be dismissed without consequence, improper behavior will escalate. Establish a protocol for discipline: first warning, second warning, and so on. If disruptive behavior persists, you may need to speak with a parent.

- Use appropriate techniques for keeping the participants focused and for channeling their energy (see Catechist Tip Sheets 2 and 5).

- Encourage the young people to assume positions of responsibility—as readers, prayer leaders, recorders, and so on. The more engaged they are, the more likely they are to behave appropriately.

- Positive begets positive. Recognize and affirm appropriate behavior. Young adolescents seek recognition and truly want to do the right thing. Encourage them when they do.

- In extreme cases, seek help. Some people have emotional and behavioral issues that require special handling. When encountering such a situation, seek help from the program coordinator or pastor immediately.

Catechist Tip Sheet 5

Helping Young Adolescents to Pay Attention

Catechists working with young adolescents face the challenge of capturing and keeping the participants' attention during sessions. A "wondering mind" and a short attention span is natural during adolescence. In addition, some youth have Attention Deficit Disorder (ADD) or Attention Deficit Hyperactivity Disorder (ADHD) and face even greater challenges paying attention than their peers.

Most young adolescents want to remain focused and connected to the group. When they aren't successful, be a guide and mentor. Suspend judgment and try different techniques. Convey to them your belief that they are capable young people and that with the right strategies and support, they can manage their own behavior. This empowering approach will result in better attention and more learning!

If you know that a participant has ADD or ADHD, you can talk to his or her parents or guardians and learn what techniques they find helpful at home and in school. In addition, the following strategies can help you facilitate learning by enhancing the attention of all adolescents, not just those with attention issues.

Attention-Enhancing Strategies

- Create order.
- Limit visual distractions.
- Be flexible about seating.
- Use smaller groupings.
- Give regular breaks.
- Communicate in more than one way.
- Check for understanding.
- Give step-by-step instructions.

Arranging Your Meeting Space

Create order and limit visual distractions. Use window shades to block out stimuli from outdoors and reduce distractibility. Keep the meeting space organized: use boxes or bags to keep supplies out of sight until needed.

Consider alternative seating. Some young people focus better when seated in the front, but some do better when seated in the back, on the side, or standing or sitting on the floor. Be flexible and let the participants choose the postures that work best for them.

Downsize. In group settings, taking turns answering questions can make focusing difficult if there is a long listening time. Try small groupings of two or three, or solicit only three "sample" responses from larger groups.

Allow breaks. Young adolescents need frequent breaks. Short breaks that allow them to stand, stretch, or walk around the room can help reduce stress and increase focus.

Catechist Tip Sheet 5: Permission to reproduce is granted. © 2009 by Saint Mary's Press.

Giving Instructions

Use multiple modes. Using multiple communication techniques enables catechists to reach more learners. Keep in mind that some young people focus best by listening, some by watching, and some by doing. Write instructions on the board, but also demonstrate the steps as you read the instructions aloud.

Communicate one step at a time. Young people may have difficulty retaining multistep instructions. Communicate steps one at a time, allowing the participants to complete each step before going on to the next, or provide a written reference on the board or an index card.

Check for understanding. After you give instructions, check for understanding. Use prompts such as "Who can tell me what we're going to do next?" Avoid questions with yes or no answers, such as "Does everyone understand?" Some participants might think they understand when they do not.

Helping Young People Who Are Distracted Bring Themselves Back into Focus

Despite all your efforts, some young people may still become distracted. Avoid embarrassing them; gently invite them back into focus using these subtle techniques:

Note physical proximity. Walking close by can refocus youth who are "lost in thought." Integrate this into your natural movement so it is not seen as a "disciplinary" action.

Create personal signals. A personal "signal" is a phrase or action agreed upon in advance by you and a young person to alert him or her to refocus. Examples include a statement like "Think about this . . ." or an action such as a hand on the shoulder or a finger snap.

(These tips are drawn from the "Strategies for Helping Young People to Pay Attention" section of the introduction to the catechist guides in the Catholic Connections program. Copyright © 2009 by Saint Mary's Press. All rights reserved.)

Catechist Tip Sheet 6

Using the Scriptures

There was a time when many Catholics felt discouraged from reading the Scriptures for fear of misinterpreting them. Today the Church encourages regular use of the Bible and even serious study of it among all Catholics. The Scriptures play a critical role in our faith growth as a source of inspiration, celebration, education, and formation. The Bible both challenges and comforts those who read and reflect on it.

As a catechist you should become comfortable with using the Scriptures, and should nurture such comfort in young people. If your experience with the Bible is limited, be honest about that with the young people in your groups. Tell them that you want to grow along with them in understanding this special book and making it a part of your life.

Objectives for Adolescent Biblical Literacy

Aim to help the young people do the following:
- feel comfortable reading the Bible and exploring it with others
- understand the structure of the Bible, recognize that it is a library of various kinds of literature, and have a sense of its origins
- become familiar with the major places, people, and events in the Bible, and their order and significance in salvation history
- develop the basic skills that allow them to explore the Bible and to locate passages
- grow in their appreciation of the role of the Scriptures in the Church's life, particularly in its liturgy
- deepen their reverence and affection for the Scriptures, be open to future Bible study, and desire to make the Bible a growing part of their spiritual lives
- understand the important role context plays in interpreting the meaning of a Scripture story or passage

Catechist Tip Sheet 6: Permission to reproduce is granted. © 2009 by Saint Mary's Press.

Ways to Use the Scriptures in Faith Formation

- Use the Scriptures as part of prayer experiences and involve the participants in proclaiming the Scriptures.
- Use the Scriptures as the focus of study. Dedicate sessions to learning about biblical people and events, or apply biblical stories and lessons to the faith themes being studied.
- Use the Scriptures to make connections with the liturgy. Highlight any links between the Lectionary readings for the upcoming Sunday and the topic you are teaching.
- Use the Scriptures to make a point. Mention favorite Bible stories or verses in your presentations and even in your casual conversation.
- Use activities that increase familiarity with the Scriptures: Bible search activities, Bible games, Scripture scavenger hunts, and so on.
- Look to the Scriptures for guidance when discussing life issues. Encourage the young people to read the Scriptures and to reflect on the meaning for their lives.

Hints for Using the Scriptures Effectively

- Designate one Bible as the *group* Bible. The way you use this group Bible should convey the special nature of the Scriptures and should show reverence and respect for them.
- Display the group Bible on a prayer table in a special way. Place it on a book stand with a candle, a cross, or other symbols, but do not clutter the display.
- Involve the young people in proclaiming the Scriptures. Practice with them in advance to ensure they are adequately prepared; the Scriptures can lose much of their power if read poorly.
- Make Bibles available for all the young people. Avoid making the participants feel too formal in their use of *personal* copies of the Scriptures. They should treat their personal Bibles as they would a treasured book for study and enjoyment.

PARENT
Tip Sheet 1

Developmental Characteristics of Young Adolescents

Adolescence is a critical time of identity formation. With the onset of puberty comes an explosion of growth—physical, intellectual, emotional, social, moral, and spiritual. Understanding the nature and scope of adolescent development and responding appropriately requires patience, empathy, and a sense of humor. Young people "progress" through adolescence, no two following the same pathway. Most sixth graders show signs of emerging traits, while many eighth graders exhibit more pronounced characteristics. The characteristics listed on this tip sheet are descriptors, not predictors.

As a parent or guardian, you are the *primary* influence in your child's life during the formative years of early adolescence, regardless of what she or he may say. Your child needs you to stay engaged in her or his life while also giving her or him space to grow. Communication is the key: listen and keep the conversations going. Whether serious or silly, conversation matters!

Physical

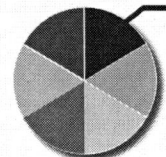

- experience onset of puberty, develop secondary sex characteristics
- grow rapidly, are often clumsy and uncoordinated
- become highly self-conscious, body image can affect self-image
- fluctuate between hyperactivity and lethargy
- need physical activity

Cognitive-Intellectual

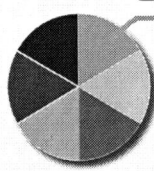

- develop ability to think abstractly, but many still think in literal terms
- develop critical thinking skills and become more self-aware, self-critical
- exhibit increased communication skills
- become argumentative and demonstrate an intense need to be "right"
- develop decision-making skills and want a voice in their choices
- show intense focus on a new interest but lack discipline to sustain it

Emotional

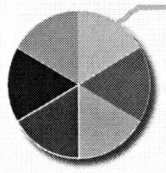

- are unpredictable emotionally, are sensitive and prone to outbursts
- are vulnerable to emotional pleas and can be easily manipulated
- exhibit an increasing capacity for empathy
- experience increasing sexual feelings, may engage in sexual behavior without realizing consequences

Parent Tip Sheet 1: Permission to reproduce is granted. © 2009 by Saint Mary's Press.

Social-Interpersonal

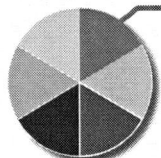

- display a more developed social consciousness
- are more aware of relationships and have a strong need to belong
- exhibit desire for independence and autonomy
- experience a shift in dependence on family to dependence on peers
- able to critically compare parents with others
- seek deeper friendships based on shared interests, loyalty
- experience increased interest in opposite sex, though may often feel uncomfortable and awkward with the other sex

Moral

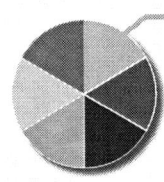

- tend to be legalistic, focusing on "rules" and "fairness"
- retain moral beliefs of parents but begin to test rules of childhood
- are influenced by the values of peers
- form a more personal conscience, seek moral criteria that make sense to them
- exhibit a stronger sense of responsibility toward larger society

Spiritual

- exhibit "affiliative faith" (faith identity shaped by family and community)
- are open to service opportunities primarily to connect with peers, test skills
- can be open to new prayer experiences
- seek adult role models who live their faith authentically
- desire a deeper relationship with God
- begin moving away from religious imagery, beliefs, and practices of childhood; may begin to explore new images of God

Being an Empathetic Parent

- In which areas of development is your child strong? struggling? How can you support his or her growth or express understanding for his or her struggles?

- Recall what it was like to be her or his age. What is it like for her or him today? How can you relate? What is different?

- Years from now, when your child reflects on his or her teen years, how will he or she remember you? How does your child's relationship with you help to shape his or her identity and beliefs?

PARENT
Tip Sheet 2

Three Key Family Faith Activities

The family is a primary influence on faith maturity during adolescence. Three key family activities can strengthen the faith growth of youth. Engaging in these activities together as a family is more powerful than young people simply observing their parents modeling religious behaviors.

Key Family Faith Activities
- Faith Conversations
- Rituals and Devotions
- Outreach and Service

Family Faith Conversations

The frequency of family faith conversations is tied to greater faith maturity in adolescents. Find ways to talk about experiences of God's presence and the joy of Christian living, as well as questions, doubts, and struggles of faith.

- Be aware of the "talkative" time of day for your child and invite discussions then.
- Maximize teachable moments that connect life and faith—patience while waiting in line, courage when facing challenges, and so on.
- Talk about teachings of the Church in relation to current events.
- Share your experiences of Church when you were young, and how faith impacts your life. Allow your child to question you about your beliefs.
- Use media as conversation starters: "What do you think about the choices made in that TV show? What might Jesus say?"
- Choose a Christian "value of the week" (e.g., forgiveness, compassion, generosity) and discuss how family members experience it.
- Read parables from the Scriptures and talk about them. Describe how Jesus might tell the stories today.
- Write sentence starters on index cards, and randomly draw one to begin a faith conversation. Here are a few examples:
  - ▶ If I could ask Jesus one question right now, I would ask . . .
  - ▶ If God wrote a text message to the world, it would say . . .
  - ▶ The hardest part about being a Christian this week was . . .

Parent Tip Sheet 2: Permission to reproduce is granted. © 2009 by Saint Mary's Press.

Family Rituals and Devotions

Many families share rituals and traditions for holidays, birthdays, and other significant life events. Establishing "faith" traditions throughout the year keeps the family grounded and growing spiritually. Add a faith dimension to existing family traditions, or develop new patterns for acknowledging the sacred in everyday life.

- Celebrate the ethnic religious traditions from your own cultural heritage.
- Establish a simple morning blessings exchange:
    - **Parent:** "May God bless and guide us this day."
    - **Adolescent:** "May we appreciate God's blessings in the people we meet."
- Set up a regular time for family prayer. Ask your child to help plan and lead prayer.
- Create a prayer intention space (bulletin board, notebook, or basket) and invite family members to post prayer intentions.
- Post a key Scripture passage on the refrigerator each week as a family spiritual focus. Here is an example:
    - "I will be with you always, to the end of the age" (Matthew 28:20).

Family Outreach and Service

Helping people in need is part of human nature and a primary message of the Gospel. Find ways to engage in service as a family and talk about the experience together.

- Allow your adolescent to choose an activity. Ideas include delivering food to people in need, cleaning out closets and donating items, and promoting recycling.
- Combine service with a fun event and join with other families. Ideas include cleaning up a park and celebrating with a picnic, and hosting a "Baking Showdown" by making favorite cookies and donating them to a soup kitchen.
- Learn about the principles of Catholic social teaching. Highlight one each month and find ways to practice it as a family.
- Talk about stewardship and the family budget. Discuss how family members use their time, talents, and treasures.
- Perform random acts of kindness and talk about the experiences together.

Acknowledgments

All scriptural quotations in this publication are from the Good News Translation in Today's English Version, Second Edition. Copyright © 1992 by the American Bible Society. Used with permission.

The excerpt on page 7 is from the English translation of the *Catechism of the Catholic Church* for use in the United States of America, second edition, number 25. Copyright © 1994 by the United States Catholic Conference, Inc.—Libreria Editrice Vaticana. English translation of the *Catechism of the Catholic Church: Modifications from the Editio Typica* copyright © 1997 by the United States Catholic Conference, Inc.—Libreria Editrice Vaticana.

The excerpts on pages 9, 12, and 18 are from the *National Directory for Catechesis,* by the United States Conference of Catholic Bishops (USCCB) (Washington, DC: USCCB, 2005), pages 202–203, 94, and 72, respectively. Copyright © 2005 by the USCCB.

The excerpt on page 10 is from *Renewing the Vision: A Framework for Catholic Youth Ministry,* by the USCCB (Washington, DC: USCCB, 1997), page 30. Copyright © 1997 by the USCCB.

The excerpt on page 14 is from *Apostolic Exhortation "Catechesi Tradendae" of His Holiness John Paul II On Catechesis In Our Time,* number 68, at *www.vatican.va/holy_father/john_paul_ii/apost_exhortations/documents/hf_jp-ii_exh_16101979_catechesi-tradendae_en.html,* accessed September 11, 2008.

The information on Catechist Tip Sheets 1 and 2 and Parent Tip Sheet 1 is from *Discovering: Coordinator's Manual,* by Thomas Zanzig with Brian Singer-Towns (Winona, MN: Saint Mary's Press, 1999), pages 72–76, 63–71, and 72–76, respectively. Copyright © 1999 by Saint Mary's Press. All rights reserved.

The information on Catechist Tip Sheets 3, 4, and 6 is from *Discovering: Teacher's Training Manual,* by Thomas Zanzig (Winona, MN: Saint Mary's Press, 1999), pages 52–55, 47–51, and 56–59, respectively. Copyright © 1999 by Saint Mary's Press. All rights reserved.

The information on Catechist Tip Sheet 5 is drawn from the "Strategies for Helping Young People to Pay Attention" section of the introduction to the catechist guides in the Catholic Connections program. Copyright © 2009 by Saint Mary's Press. All rights reserved.

To view copyright terms and conditions for Internet materials cited here, log on to the home pages for the referenced Web sites.

During this book's preparation, all citations, facts, figures, names, addresses, telephone numbers, Internet URLs, and other pieces of information cited within were verified for accuracy. The authors and Saint Mary's Press staff have made every attempt to reference current and valid sources, but we cannot guarantee the content of any source, and we are not responsible for any changes that may have occurred since our verification. If you find an error in, or have a question or concern about, any of the information or sources listed within, please contact Saint Mary's Press.

Endnote Cited in a Quotation from the *Catechism of the Catholic Church,* Second Edition

1. *Roman Catechism,* Preface, 10; cf. 1 *Cor* 13:8.

You will find additional resources to support your use of the Catholic Connections program at

www.smp.org/eSource

Click on the Catholic Connections button and you will find additional resources for program coordinators and catechists. Included in these resources are
- program planning resources
- catechist training resources
- tip sheets for catechists and parents
- downloadable handouts with activities you can use in class or send home
- additional seasonal activities appropriate for young adolescents
- links to Catholic Web sites with helpful information